Michael

"When I die, it will be in a big way, and it will change the world"

As told by Nancy Cimei

AuthorHouse™
1663 Liberty Drive
Bloomington, IN 47403
www.authorhouse.com
Phone: 833-262-8899

Because of the dynamic nature of the Internet, any web addresses or links contained in this book may have changed since publication and may no longer be valid. The views expressed in this work are solely those of the author and do not necessarily reflect the views of the publisher, and the publisher hereby disclaims any responsibility for them.

Any people depicted in stock imagery provided by Getty Images are models, and such images are being used for illustrative purposes only.
Certain stock imagery © Getty Images.

This book is printed on acid-free paper.

ISBN: 978-1-4343-8908-4 (sc)

Library of Congress Control Number: 2008904501

Print information available on the last page.

Published by AuthorHouse 10/21/2024

authorHOUSE®

This Book is Dedicated to my Granddaughters
Vanessa Michael and Adrianna Rose
with All My Love

CHAPTER 1

September 11, 2001, 8:46 am, American Airlines Flight 11 crashes into the North Tower of the World Trade Center. Astonishingly, we all look on. Only minutes later, United Airlines Flight 175 flies down the same path, circles around the south side of Manhattan and crashes into the South Tower. It was 9:03 am.

Now the world looks on in fear and anger. My heart beating so fast, I wonder if Michael could be there. But deep within my soul I know the truth. At 9:08, Ladder 35, on the upper west side of Manhattan, gets the call to respond and just moments later Engine 40, from the same house, also responds. Michael rides down with six other men on the engine to what would be only his second fire. It was also his last. This becomes the saddest day of my life. This is the day my son Michael died.

Every parent knows their child to be the best. Loving them unconditionally. Proud of them for their accomplishments no matter how small. This is just one story, of one son, by me, his mom. A story that needed to be told about a son taken much before his time. A son taken much before I was willing to accept. A son who was warm and kind, funny, hard working, generous, caring and loved by all he touched.

Monday, February 16, 1976, 11:30 am, became one of the best moments of my life. It is the moment I was blessed with a baby boy. His name was Michael D'Auria. I remember the nurses in the hospital telling me how he was smiling in the delivery room and how rare that was. I somehow knew at that moment how special Michael would be.

Michael came home from the hospital to a beautiful big sister waiting for him. Christina was 3 years and 10 months older and adored her baby brother. She would crawl right behind Michael when he was learning to crawl just to hear him laugh. They played so well together. And he was such a good baby. That is until the age of three. Michael never seemed to go through those terrible two's everyone talks about. But boy did he make up for it by the time he turned three years old. At that point he never wanted to sleep. At least not until maybe two in the morning. But luckily for me that time did pass.

Michael and Christina were very close growing up although almost four years apart in age. Michael was born and raised for the first five years of his life in Brooklyn, New York. Then Michael's dad and I, along with our precious children, moved to Staten Island. Four months after we moved Michael began kindergarten. By now his very blonde hair was starting to fade away and the golden brown hair was starting to make a presence. He and his sister Christina were not very happy over the move since they left behind many friends where we had lived in Brooklyn. But my children were resilient and it didn't take long before they made new acquaintances. I can't begin to count how many friends Michael made as a child.

His early years in school went well. And since we lived across the street from their school, PS 32, I used to tease the kids and tell them they needed to have 102 temperature in order to stay home - no excuses.
At one point I remember the principal calling me on the telephone. "Mrs. D'Auria", she said, "Michael must stop". She let me know that he was in the schoolyard at play or lunch time watching for bullies who were bothering other kids. At the time the Guardian Angels had become known in New York City and Michael felt the need to emulate what they were known for. Protect those who couldn't protect themselves.

The rest of grammar school was pretty uneventful. He played T-ball and baseball for Great Kills Little League. My son loved being outdoors, and playing handball in the schoolyard down the block, but riding his bicycle gave him the freedom he wanted to explore our neighborhood, within reason, of course.

As he approached his teen years Michael needed eyeglasses. He also was given a key to the house so when he came home from school, if I was late getting home from work, he would let himself in the house. But there was a period of time when my son was the 'absent minded professor'. Eyeglasses and keys were replaced on a regular basis. Eyeglasses were sometimes found but never in a condition to be worn again.

After grammar school Michael went on to Intermediate School 75, which was a three year school. He was never happier. He had such a terrific group of friends, and now he was not only friends with the boys but with the girls. My phone never stopped ringing and Michael became Mr. Popularity. He actually had it tough when they graduated, knowing they'd be splitting up to attend different high schools.

It was also a difficult time for Michael since his dad and I were getting divorced. Michael attended Susan Wagner High School in the ninth grade but missed his friends and his dad. So in the summer of 1991 he went down to Florida to visit his father for two weeks. When he came back I could see by the look on his face there was something he needed to tell me. Michael asked to move to Florida to be with his dad. This was a shock for me. But the more I thought about it the more I realized I needed to allow him to do this. He was fifteen and he needed his dad. Michael attended Boyd Anderson High School in Fort Lauderdale, Florida for one year and during that time was the catcher for his baseball team. I did visit him with Christina at Thanksgiving time, staying with my parents who had a condo nearby. And before we knew it Michael came home for Christmas. Then I visited again in March and by the time Easter vacation came about Michael was begging to come home. So June 14 at 12 noon Michael finished his sophomore year and at 4 pm he was on a plane headed for New York to stay. I knew I did the right thing. Michael and I became closer than ever. He then attended St. Joseph by the Sea High School for the next two years graduating in June, 1994.

Although my son was very smart he could not sit still. He always had much energy so the thought of going to college was not making him happy. After seeing photograph's from a friend's cruise vacation and a beautifully decorated buffet, Michael thought he should attend culinary school. I thought it a little odd since he never attempted to cook at home. But one week after high school graduation he entered the New York Restaurant School in Manhattan. After completing his course he worked at Gabriel's in Manhattan, Chadwick's in Brooklyn, La Fontana and Giovanni's Cafe on Staten Island. He was an excellent chef who truly loved his time in the kitchen. And even more than cooking he loved to make desserts. No one could make a creme brulee' like Mike. Anytime I went to dinner at the restaurant he would have a creme brulee' ready for me.

Michael was extremely close to his sister Christina, especially at three in the morning when he'd ring her bell and ask to borrow a $20 bill. And he'd always ask me for approval on an idea he had - just to see if he was making the right decision. Except when he told me some ten years later how he had sneaked out one night and slept on the school roof. These are some of the things we smile about now when we think about Michael.

Over the next seven years, while working as a chef, Michael took the written test for the Fire Department of New York. I'll never forget the time I was on vacation and he called to tell me he scored 100% on the test. I was so excited for him I cried. This was the career my son wanted since he was a little boy.

Over the next couple of years Michael had much work to do. The gym was a must and so, like the written test, he took the physical test and also received 100%. He was so happy I thought he would bust. He also needed to have lasik surgery in order to correct his vision and thirty college credits to join the FDNY. So to night school he went.

In the beginning of 2001 Michael knew he was going to be called for the job soon. He also knew there wouldn't be a vacation for a while, so along with two friends, both of whom firefighters already, a vacation was planned. Michael always knew how to spend his money. He never learned how to save. Three days into a four/five day vacation he called me and asked (begged) me to wire him another five hundred dollars. He said, "Mom I'm having the best time of my life, please?" So against my better judgment, I did. Now when I think back I'm so happy that I did. That was Michael's last vacation. That was his friend Rob's last vacation also.

On May 2, 2001 Michael was sworn in to the FDNY to begin his eight weeks of training at the Fire Academy on Randall's Island. During his time at the Fire Academy my son came home with all the equipment necessary to start his career as a firefighter. Bunker gear, helmet, boots and so much more. He needed to work in the restaurant that night and had been so excited about the fire department, so he completely dressed from head to toe in all his gear and drove himself to work so all could see. They loved Michael at Giovanni's and were so sad to see him leave, but were really happy to know he was moving on to the career he had always dreamed of.

On July 6, 2001, after training at Probie School, he was assigned to Ladder 35 and Engine 40 on the upper west side of Manhattan. Michael loved Manhattan and he loved the fire department so this was the perfect combination. One Saturday night I received a message from Michael's firehouse to call the 'house' if he gets in within the hour. When Michael arrived home some 10 minutes later I gave him the message. He called the firehouse and it seems they needed the recipe for a sauce he made them a couple of weeks earlier.

The new probationary firefighters were to do seven weeks with the Engine and then seven weeks with the Truck (Hook & Ladder) or the reverse, after which time the probies would go back to Randall's Island for three more weeks of CPR review and then Graduation. Only something went wrong.

Michael had completed only nine of the fourteen weeks. On Sunday morning, September 9 when my son awoke I asked him what he had planned for the day. He said he was attending a Fund Raiser for deceased firefighters. That was the last conversation I had with my son. That evening, when I came back from the movies, I noticed Michael's duffle bag was not in his room. Michael was working the next two days and like other times had decided to sleep at the firehouse the night before and cook dinner for the men on the night tour. I don't know who enjoyed that more, Michael or the guys. Monday's tour was rather routine and after work he and another probie friend went to Brooklyn to watch Monday night football and get a bite to eat. They talked about working in Manhattan and having to go into hi-rise buildings. But Michael said it didn't matter to him because he joined the FDNY to save lives. Michael slept at the firehouse again that night and started his tour at 9 am. Just one hour later one fireman was severely injured from Ladder 35/Engine 40 and twelve others would never return.

November 1, 2001 was Michael's official graduation day. I received his diploma posthumously.

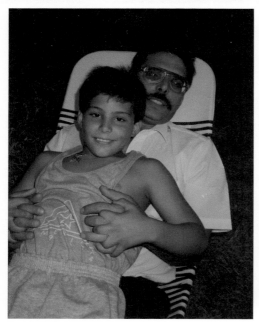

CHAPTER 2

Sometime during his teen years my son got his first tattoo. Knowing how I felt about them, there was no doubt he would keep this from me. At least until summer came when shorts and bathing suits were worn. The first tattoo was tribal in nature, a red and black face on the outside of his left calf. But this was only the beginning. That same summer, while Mike was wearing flip-flops, a friend noticed an EYE tattooed on his big toe. When she asked what that was Michael replied, "My mom always tells me 'Michael, watch your step'." Michael did have a sense of humor.

Sometime later I was giving my son a haircut and he needed to take off his tee shirt to brush off. Well lo and behold, St. Michael the Archangel was on his right shoulder blade. He said he needed him there to protect him.

When Michael had finished culinary school and was working in Manhattan on the upper west side, he would leave work around 1 am and wait close to an hour for the train to take him down to the ferry. Once there he would wait for the ferry to Staten Island which was a twenty to twenty five minute ride then have to wait for the Staten Island Rapid Transit (the train that would take him to our town) sometimes another half hour or so. This trip would take him two to three hours every night, only to wake up each morning and start all over again. So at the age of nineteen Michael moved out. He decided Queens would be the best choice. One train, fifteen minutes and he'd be at work. When his job took him to Brooklyn he moved to Brooklyn. By the time Michael was twenty four years old he decided to make another move. Rents were getting to be too much for him and knowing the fire department would be hiring him soon he would have to tighten his belt.

While a probationary firefighter you were only allowed to work that one job and pay started out very low. So in September, 2000, Michael moved back home, so he wouldn't have to pay rent, and at that point was working nearby our home. I was elated. I had my son back home with me.

Michael came home one night, showered and went out but somehow I knew he was up to something. Mother's never seem to lose that sense. Tattoo #4 was in the making. Outside my parents' apartment, which was downstairs from me, was a statue of St. Anthony that they brought with them from Brooklyn. Every time Michael would leave from their apartment he'd touch St. Anthony. Then he would make the sign of the cross. This had become a turning point in his life. He had begun reading a lot, many of the books being books of spiritual guidance. This one particular morning, when Michael awoke, I noticed the large bandage on his right forearm, so I asked him where he had gone the previous night after work. Well he removed the bandage and from his elbow to his wrist was St. Anthony.

Don't get me wrong not that there is anything wrong with St. Anthony, but I was shocked at the size of it. Well I was proud of myself, my mouth remained open but nothing came out. When your child works hard and has reached the age of twenty four, as he was when he got this tattoo, sometimes you just need to know when not to say anything, especially when they are not positive comments.

Over the next few months he went and had the rest of his forearm filled in with cherubs and a waving ribbon with the serenity prayer written on the ribbon. At the time I just never thought about why. Now that I look back I feel somehow he was preparing for something greater.

Michael always lived his life to the fullest, as if it were his last day on earth. He needed to get it all in. He spent his salary faster than he earned it. Being a chef with a good heart he'd take friends to expensive

Manhattan restaurants to try new cuisines and cultures. We would always tell him to slow down. You need to start saving. You go to extremes. I can't tell you how happy I am today that he did all these things. I believe that he did need to get it all in because here his time was limited.

In the beginning of the year 2001, a friend of Michael's showed him a painting from an art magazine. It was a beautiful painting of a swimmer underwater and it appeared to be a young man from the early 1900's. Sabrina really admired this painting but admitted that it was too expensive for her to purchase. So Michael, always looking to make people happy, said he would paint it for her. She said, "I had no idea you painted". Mike admitted to her that he didn't but he also assured her he would be able to paint this picture. Well Michael talked her into going with him for supplies and there began his very short lived career as an artist. Within a couple of weeks Michael had his first painting completed and very proudly handed it to her.

But Michael held on to this art magazine and within the next couple of weeks presented me with a beautiful painting of an Angel from this same magazine. I was so amazed. Nothing like this was ever done by my son. I knew he had a sense of creativity, but we believed it to be shown in the culinary delights he prepared. He always made sure he would prepare his own plate for dinner so that he could arrange the food in a creative way.

Well not long after I received my painting I noticed that Michael was working on his third one. A painting for his sister Christina. A boy and girl playing leapfrog in a field. The only thing was that it was Christina's birthday in April and she did not receive her gift until June. He would tell her that her present wasn't ready yet but never told her what the present was going to be. Believe it or not I never realized how much of a perfectionist my son was until then, because the painting was complete but Mike was unhappy with a part of it and would not present it to Christina until he felt it was perfect.

One evening I came home from work and there was Michael sitting at our kitchen counter painting his fourth painting and listening to Andrea Bocelli. I could not believe I was watching my son. He never ceased to amaze me. I took a picture of Michael's gift to his friend and had it enlarged and matted then gave it to him so he would always have his own copy. Now I have that wonderful part of my son hanging in my home along with my Angel. The fourth painting, also hanging in my home, is an abstract of three faces, incomplete.

The following books were read by Michael and were the beginning of his library.

THE ROAD LESS TRAVELED	by M. Scott Peck M.D.
SEAT OF THE SOUL	by Gary Zukav
THE TIPPING POINT	by Malcolm Gladwell
INTUITIVE LIVING	by Alan Seale
FACING THE FIRE	by John Lee with Bill Stott
THE CELESTINE PROPHECY	by James Redfield
THE PORTABLE	by Carl Jung

ILLUSIONS   by Richard Bach

EMBRACED BY THE LIGHT   by Betty J. Eadie

THE POWER OF NOW   by Eckhart Talle

HOW TO KNOW GOD   by Deepak Chopra

WISDOM OF THE AGES   by Wayne W. Dyer

ESSENTIAL DALI'   by Kirsten Bradbury

THE CONSCIOUS MIND   by David Chalmers

SOUL STORIES   by Gary Zukav

MANY LIVES, MANY MASTERS   by Brian L. Weiss M.D

BUDDHA HEART, BUDDHA MIND   by Dalai Lama

AWAKENING THE BUDDHA WITHIN   by Lama Surya Das

SEVEN SPIRITUAL LAWS OF SUCCESS   by Deepok Chopra

ADDICTIVE THINKING &   by Abraham J. Twerski M.D.
ADDICTIVE PERSONALITY   & Craig Nakken

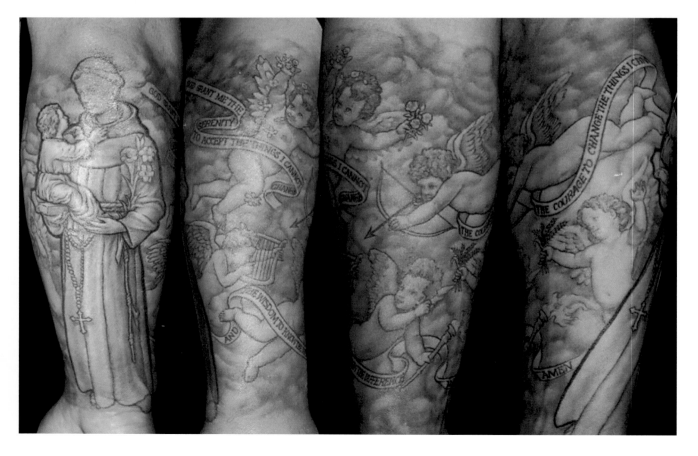

CHAPTER 3

Michael was the youngest of thirteen grandchildren on his father's side of the family, most of whom were much older than he. Since we were living on Staten Island we also were not living near to them. But on my side, he and his sister were the oldest of eight grandchildren. Five boy cousins and one girl cousin to watch over. And that's exactly what he did.

He had such a good time with them, especially when we would get together for dinner. The kids would always be laughing. He did silly things, like stick straws up his nose and make like a walrus. Or stand in a doorway with only the top half of his body showing and his arms extended as if he were flying. I laugh thinking about it because he really did look as if he were flying. He had a knack for imitating old karate movies in foreign language showing how the voices were off sinc.

I once read that our lives unfold like dominoes. Every piece that falls is an action which creates a reaction. Everything we do in our lives affects someone in some way. Even if it is not realized until much after the action or perhaps at times not at all. Each one of my nephews and niece had a special relationship with Michael.

My nephew Robert was ten years old when he needed to write an essay for school on someone he admired. Robert wrote about Michael. At that time Michael was twenty. Here is an excerpt from that essay: "He loves everyone and thinks nobody should have a bad life. He never hates anyone. He respects other people and himself. I love him because of those things."

In a letter Robert wrote me he said "I miss Michael terribly. I feel like I lost my older brother. We talk every day. He's always with me. Thank you for bringing Michael into this world." In November of 2001 Robert was diagnosed with acute myeloid leukemia (AML). He spent six months in the hospital having intense chemotherapy, spinal taps, blood tests and so much more. We thank God he is now cancer free. He says "From what I have been through and all I have experienced I have learned that you can't take little things for granted and every moment must be cherished, because this thing we call life, is way too precious". Robert never ever complained. He did say he believed he had been given this illness to help our family cope with the loss of Michael. Strangely, I do understand what he means. We put all our energy into helping my sister, brother-in-law and their three sons in any way we could. So while trying to heal over the loss of Michael, physically we kept ourselves very busy.

My niece Stefanie recalls at every family affair, when Michael walked in he put a smile on every single face there. Her best memories of Michael are on the special holidays. "We would sit down to eat dinner and even at twenty five years old, Michael would be sitting at the "kiddy" table. He was usually playing jokes on Thomas and making us laugh so hard we could hardly breathe."

Stefanie told me her funniest memory of Michael was when he worked as a chef at Giovanni's Café. She would see him from time to time standing outside the side door of the kitchen during his break. Stef had a friend who lived down that same street so whenever she would walk with her friend passed the restaurant she would look for Michael in order to see his "big smile" and give him a big hug and kiss. His famous words to her were "be careful, and try not to get into too much trouble" which was quite funny since Stef never got into trouble.

One particular night she spotted him from afar but also noticed there were two other workers with Michael. Apparently he was making a bet with them (which he would do often enough) that he could get this girl's telephone number, not realizing yet that this girl was his cousin. (Obviously, this was before his lasik surgery.) When he finally realized, as she came a bit closer, he first turned beet red. The others realized it was Stefanie and got hysterical. Michael told her about the bet and was laughing at himself, but she said "I don't think I ever saw him get so embarrassed".

In so many ways my nephew Danny, Stefanie's younger brother, reminds me of my son. Very warm and loving, as they all are, but always on the go and has the greatest hugs. He remembers playing handball with Michael in the school yard. Mike would show him the "correct way" to play. And when they were finished playing they would walk back to my brother's house and Michael would talk to Danny. I say talk 'to' instead of 'with' because that's just what he did. Since Michael was older and working, the kids didn't see him too often, so my son made sure that Danny and his other cousins always knew he would be there for them, giving them advice and reassuring his love for them.

Thomas tells me of the time Michael asked him if he wanted to take a ride to the city with him while he was to get one of his tattoos. Michael had said, "I'll beep you when I'm outside". Thomas was surprised Michael wasn't coming in to see the rest of his family. Later he found out that Mike wasn't ready to hear from Aunt Angela and Uncle Bobby about why he shouldn't get another tattoo. Tommy was surprised when instead Michael did ring the bell. When Tommy opened the door my son said, "I was about to beep but I remembered I don't have a horn". Thomas says Michael was the type of guy who didn't care whether he drove a "Benz or an '86 Buick. And that's how he lived his life. Taking what came his way and dealing with it. Not complaining and not just accepting, but being grateful for what he had.

"Michael was more than just a friend to everyone. When we lost him we lost a part of ourselves." Thomas continues to say "I can't help but think about the times I almost passed out because he made me laugh so hard at something ridiculous he would do". If Michael was at our family party the kids knew it would be a night full of laughing and eating really good chocolate chip cookies. Of course they almost had to beg Mike to make them. But in a way it made them taste better seeing how they might not get them for who knew how long.

On September 7, 2001, Michael took Thomas into the city again. This time to show him around, get a bite to eat and just spend time together. Michael bought Tommy records for his new DJ equipment and so they spent a good portion of the day enjoying each other's company. No matter what it was they wanted, Michael made sure he would be there to support his cousins. He helped them and encouraged them in anyway possible. Everyone who knew Michael knew this about him. Always giving and doing for others. Always worrying about others first. So when he passed away running in to the World Trade Center, helping in the way that he did, no one was surprised.

Mike made everything look so easy. When he talked, people listened, but when he wasn't talking, that is when people listened the most. You could learn a lot from Michael by just watching him and acknowledging him. His words were powerful and they stuck with you. The way he viewed everything was so different than anyone else. He was a chef, an artist, a firefighter. He was a son, brother, grandson, nephew and cousin, but most of all best friend and this was all at the young age of 25. He always said if you want to do something, do it! Stop saying it and just do it. What's holding you back? The mark he left with everyone he came in contact with was indescribable. And that is the way he lived his short but amazing life.

It was easy for Stefanie, Robert, Danny and Tommy to tell me what they remembered about Michael. But for Jesse and John it was difficult. They were younger, much younger. They are disappointed in not being able to recall much more than Michael playing on the floor with them and doing silly things to make them laugh. This writing is dedicated to them also. It is a reading that will make them feel they knew Michael like the rest of us.

CHAPTER 4

Here are some of the quotes that several of Michael's friends wrote:

He was the ingredient the kitchen needed to make a perfect recipe.

We didn't have to say anything to understand one another.

I can't tell you enough how much you made a difference in everyone's lives. I know the difference you made in mine is knowing now what a hero really is. In the time I got to spend with you and things you said to me I now understand the true meaning of friendship. You're such an inspiration to me.

When Mike's name was on the board (firehouse) we knew we would eat well that night.

You are irreplaceable in the hearts you have touched.

We didn't know each other very well but as did all the other girls in the school I too had a crush on him.

Mike, I remember being there when you got your tattoo (angel) on your back and you telling me how he was going to look after you. I'm sure he is with you now, letting you know how loved and appreciated you were. I remember when you had dyed your hair platinum blonde, how you made me laugh. You are and always will be a beautiful person in my heart and mind.

You were only here with us at E-40 & L-35 for a short time, but you made more of an impression than most people make in a lifetime.

You even gave your own jacket off your back to a friend in need. Everything that I see, say and do is different because of you.

All the girls loved you in our neighborhood, and you never let it go to your head.

I count my blessings everyday for the gift of knowing Michael.

Michael, you are a true hero, not only for how you shined during our worst day, but for how you lived. Living next door to Michael was a pleasure. Michael was always respectful and helpful. Michael would watch over my son who was younger than him, like a big brother. Every time I went out to cut the grass or wash the car, Michael would come out and talk to me. We talked about a lot of things, "life, the pressures of growing up, school, work". Since I was an NYPD Officer, he always wanted to know about the police and firemen. He used to say "John you are a real hero". I used to laugh and tell him "Mike, heroes aren't made heroes, they are born heroes. Michael, I am so proud of you!! You are the TRUE HERO in my eyes.

He was like a big brother to me, he protected me.

He was the type of guy who would go to the ends of the earth to help somebody.

How he made me laugh.

You worked for me in my kitchen. You were a great kid and a hard worker. I see you in my teenaged sons and that's a good thing.

You touched my life in the way you touched so many others.

He always seemed to have a sincerity that made him unique from the others our age.

Michael believed in "connections", he believed in the power of the human soul, he believed in humanity...

He liked to listen and learn, which lead to fulfillment thru sharing.

You are greatly missed by many Mike, but we think of you and are forced to smile.

Michael was my first, best friend growing up in Brooklyn. Mike was a great guy and the best friend a kid could ever have. You are the essence of courage and a hero. You are loved and missed.

He touched my life so deeply and I will always be grateful for getting the chance to meet and get to know someone like him. He is irreplaceable and will always have a place in my heart.

I always trusted Michael and knew deep within my soul that he was special. Thank you for bringing him into this world for all of us to know. He touched many lives.

Michael taught me to savor every bite of food I ate – appreciate all colors and textures and sounds that I contacted. The world is not the same for me and I thank him for teaching me every day.

These are some of the special things that have been said about my son. Friends he knew for a long time and friends he barely knew. I thought I knew the man I raised so well but I am finding out still to this day how remarkably special he was, not only to me, his mother, and Michael's entire family but to so many more people than I could ever imagine.

A dear friend of Michael's is a writer and four years after my son's demise, Anthony wrote an article for our local newspaper. Here is an excerpt from that article.

"It was now 8 o'clock, and my girlfriend and other friends from Staten Island had called to make sure I was safe. I asked my friend, Joe, if he had been able to get in touch with Mike. He said no, but reassured me that he was fine and only playing a joke on us. We both then agreed he couldn't have been there; he was just a probie".

At the age of 25, Mike had lived a more grandiose life than those four times his age. He would sit with me for hours at work when we weren't busy, and just talk about life. On the weekends, we would go out and have the best times – dancing, talking to girls and simply having fun.

Mike was a mentor to me and I viewed him as an older brother. Sure, everyone told me what to do and I was sure they knew what they were talking about, but when Mike said it, it was real. There wasn't that much of an age gap, and for precisely that reason everything he said, I valued.

If ever I had a problem, and couldn't go to my parents, Mike was there. In fact, Mike believed in me and instilled a confidence I carry to this day. It was Mike who sat down with me and discussed where I would go to college. He explained that although I was a Staten Island All-Star in football, I had something other jocks didn't – brains. New York University became my choice over several football scholarships at other universities because he made me realize that I would have to rely on my intelligence for the rest of my life, rather than my bench press.

While he was alive, Mike always joked when we talked about the future. Neither one of us really knew what we wanted to do with the rest of our lives. One thing though that always remained constant in his prognostication was that he would one day do something so great that the entire world would know about it. He would say that some how or some way, he intended to be a hero, and have his name known worldwide.

I am proud to say that Mike fulfilled his dream. Unfortunately, it resulted in his demise, but he achieved what he set out to do. Mike is a hero known worldwide. His death, along with the deaths of so many other members of New York's Bravest, gives true definition to the word. Not a weekend goes by when something I'll do or somewhere I'll go won't remind me of the times and wisdom he shared with me. Now, as a member of the graduating class of the horrific event of 9/11, I embark on the next portion of my life's journey. Although Mike has passed, I am sure he's looking down on me, protecting and guiding my every step. Just as he helped me choose this institution verbally, I know he will help me plan out the rest of my life spiritually. I can only hope to make him proud with my choices, and to one day be a hero to someone else in the same way he was to me."

Another young man Michael befriended, Steven, had become very good friends with my son while working at Giovanni's Café as a busboy at the time Michael was the chef. This is a paper he wrote for school.

"Emily Coue' once wrote, 'Everyday, in everyway, I am getting better'." Many of us read this statement and take it at face value, without ever truly grasping the profoundness of those seven small words. I was fortunate enough to have worked with an individual who provided me with the insight to transform this quote into a template on which to construct the foundation of my life. This individual was Michael D'Auria. Even in the face of adversity, he exhibited a disposition of optimism, and was never satisfied with mediocrity. He searched daily for ways in which to better himself both as a person and as a part of society. As an adolescent, I watched Mike make decisions for his self-improvement, until his aspiration came to fruition when he became a New York City Fireman. As a probation officer, he sacrificed his life on September 11th saving others. It is because of his selfless act of heroism that people survived the devastation of that horrific event.

Clearly, on that day Mike was getting better in every way, such that his life was given to culminate what his standards of perfection were. Although his physical presence has been lost, his memory shall forever remain engraved on my heart. He has helped shape me into the individual I am today. It was his exemplary outlook on life that molded my current perspective on everyday activities.

As my recommendation letters demonstrate, I volunteer my service to the community by helping mentally disabled children. This experience has shown me what Michael had always known. That no matter how many tangible goods one may have, the feeling of intangible happiness brought about by the smile of a child is priceless.

I am heartbroken to say that Michael is not here to continue to guide me with wisdom and experience, but what he taught me earlier, has been the driving force behind my work ethic at my job, in the classroom, and on the field. Being the captain of my soccer team has allowed me to act towards my peers as Mike acted towards me. As a gentle voice that is not here to reprimand, but rather to encourage and support them. Now I find myself working to earn a masters degree in accounting and then to continue into law school. Just as Mike bettered himself every day in every way possible, so will I embark on my collegiate journey one step at a time. Each step will surpass the previous one with regard to my expectations. It is through this process of constant self-actualization that my steps will surely lead me to my destination: success and happiness."

I can only hope and pray that my son knew the impact he had on those who were so close to him.

CHAPTER 5

I don't know of anyone who hasn't experienced some time when their child didn't follow the household rules or get into some kind of trouble. We seem to believe, as a childless couple, that when we have children, "ours will be different". Well those of us who were blessed with these little angels have come to know differently. No child is perfect. We may try to instill in them respect and kindness to others, good morals and the ability to become independent caring adults but I know this doesn't always carry through. Most times but not all the time. Every family situation is different and every child becomes molded accordingly. When Michael was 14 years old and his dad and I separated, it affected my children in different ways. Christina was 18 years old and graduating high school. She was going to leave home to live at school. But Michael was young. And being male needed his dad at this very crucial age.

Well who knows your children better that their friends at this age. They are the ones they talk to. I feel lucky to have kept in contact with Mike's friends and have had on more than one occasion the pleasure of their company. Although it's difficult to see them without my son's presence I have come to know him more than I thought I had. Actually maybe more than I wanted to.

Many stories I've heard I am sure Michael would have appreciated them remaining his secret. I do know that his friends were there for him when he needed them. They were the male figures who took part in helping to make Mike who he was. He was filled with anger in the beginning of his teen years because his dad left and at times expressed himself in ways he should not have. But structure in his life by family and friends really did help in allowing him to work through his emotions.

The day before my Michael moved to Florida with his dad, Michael's friends all cut class to spend quality time with him. Michael had the idea that it should be recorded on video tape. From eating at the diner, to just driving around checking out the girls it has become a memory for them that keeps them laughing. They ended the day on the beach at Great Kills Park and when Michael spotted this young girl on the beach he took off his clothes down to his boxers and convinced her she should go in the water with him. Well off they went. So many years ago and the guys still have a good laugh. As one friend (Keith) kept saying, "Mike, the chick magnet, always a chick magnet".

Kenny recalled the time it was his sixteenth birthday, and Mike, who was only 14, approached Kenny and shook his hand to wish him a Happy Birthday. To Kenny's surprise Mike had had money in his hand. They had only been friends a short time yet Michael wanted to show him he cared by giving him something. Kenny said, "I'll never forget that, we were just kids".

Eddy recalls the time he and Michael were dressed to go out and were driving in his car. They passed two older women in their car with a flat tire. Mike told Eddy to pull over and he got out and changed the tire for them. They all agreed that they were raised to have respect, give up your seat to the elderly, help someone in need. But when the time actually arose, it always seemed they would think about doing the right thing, but it was Michael who acted on it. No hesitation.

They had a good laugh remembering the time some of them went to Action Park thinking it was half price for opening day. To their disappointment they missed opening day and had to pay full price. Michael did not have enough money nor did the other two boys. So they pooled their money together, bought two tickets and Michael convinced the girl at the window to let him in for free. They think he even got her telephone number.

"He always had a passion for everything" Steve M. said. He made you feel you were the only one in the room, no matter how many people were there. One time Michael sat in a club talking with some "geek" and when asked by a friend "Mike, what are you doing?" Michael just held up his hand as if to say "leave us, we're talking". Michael understood that everyone is important, not just the "cool" guys.

They broke into hysteria when Nicky reminded them of the night they were all out in a club and Michael came straight from working at the restaurant. He walked in with his chef's uniform on – checkered pants, white jacket and dancing. He always did what he felt, not caring about any negative opinions.

In a quieter moment they talked about how easy it was to talk with their friend. How Mike was never judgmental. If you did something you were questioning or just needed to talk he made you feel everything would be alright. You could say anything and it would be OK. Then he'd give you an entirely new perspective, a way in which you never thought of thinking about your problem.

I seemed to find out many of Michael's mischievous activities many years after the fact. Like that night he sneaked out of the house and slept on the school roof, across from where we lived. It was summer and he thought it would be cool. And I don't mean the temperature. I don't know if that's a good thing or not. All I know is that my son loved life and made sure he enjoyed himself.

Eddy had tears in his eyes telling me what Michael did after his grandfather had died. Michael would ring Eddy's bell on Sunday, then walk in the side door and call "Rae, Rae, you there"? Eddy's grandpa would call that out to his mother when he came over. Eddy said he'll never forget how Mike made his mother smile.

During the time Michael lived in Florida with his dad, he had a visit from Keith and Steve E., also known to the guys as Fud. On their first night out they were so happy to be together for spring break that Michael decided to climb a palm tree. He made it all the way to the top. So they all had to do it. Then they went to Denny's to get something to eat, something which had become a nightly ritual. Michael decided afterward, at around 3 am, that it would be a good idea to go fishing. So they went home, got their fishing rods and fished until the sun came up.

Michael took his first vacation as an adult in February 1995. He and Frank, one of his new friends from culinary school, celebrated his 19th birthday on the island of Turks and Cacoas, then met up with Steve (Fud) in Florida. Altogether they were away three weeks. This became very typical for Michael. He enjoyed going on vacation and did so as often as he could. Florida, the Islands, Greece, wherever and whenever possible.

On this particular trip the three young men stayed at Michael's dad's home. They went out to a club one evening and upon their arrival back home, quite late and feeling no pain, could not fall asleep. Michael got this crazy idea to put on his grandmother's house dresses and a wig and stockings over their heads. They had a blast singing and dancing while everyone else in the house was asleep (well at least trying to sleep).

Another night Michael wanted a challenge. He thought it might be fun to see if he could get himself inside the clothes dryer. So he crammed himself in and Steve took a picture of him coming out. Steve says he always had that great sense of humor. He also always had the girls, so Steve would borrow his clothes because Mike had the "cool stuff".

During another one of their vacations, on a visit to Key West, they had decided to rent scooters. At the end of the day Steve fell off doing around 35 mph. He hit the street and slid about 30 feet. He got up and Mike quickly moved him out of the way of oncoming traffic. Michael then ran over to a houseboat to try to get water and first aid. The entire time he was laughing as was Steve, only in much pain. On their way home that evening Michael needed to drive. Well, Michael didn't know how to drive a stick shift. (Steve had rented the car). Steve tried to stay awake but fell asleep and woke up to Mike going from 5th gear to 1st gear because he needed to stop and didn't know how. When he finally did come to a stop, Steve shot forward into the windshield. They had to drive the rest of the way back in 3rd gear. To Steve, Michael made it funny somehow and they went on with the vacation after getting the car fixed. Steve said, "I never would have had so much fun on vacations if Mike wasn't part of it. He always made it a good time and made people around him laugh. I will never forget those memories and the friend he was to me."

CHAPTER 6

Michael tried in so many ways to make the people around him happy by fulfilling their lives. Knowing that his Nanny loved the Yankees he bought tickets to a Yankee game and took her to her first major league game. She was in her mid seventies at the time and just the two of them went together. Besides taking his cousin to the city when he went for a tattoo, because he knew it was the only quality time they had, he took the young busboys from the restaurant where he worked to see the Staten Island Yankees. And bowling with all of them after work instead of going out with the guys.

Michael assumed responsibility for those around him too. While working in the kitchen of one of the restaurants, he had a conversation with a fellow chef and friend, I'll call Joe. Joe was having a problem with substance abuse and told Michael that his girlfriend was now pregnant. So Michael took off a quite expensive wrist watch he had been wearing, gave it to Joe and told him "Every time you look at your new watch, remember how much time you have left to straighten out your life before your baby is born". He made it a point of letting those around him know just how much he cared.

In yet another restaurant, the guys set up a football pool for the Superbowl. Now while I admit I don't completely understand how this works, I do know that there was only one box left to buy (bet on). Since it was quite an expensive one, finding someone to fill it was not easy. Then Michael heard that a friend and his dad were interested so he went and made the necessary introductions. They purchased this last box and watched the Superbowl with great anxiety. Well, they won. They won over one hundred thousand dollars. He went to their home, knocked on the door and joined them in their wild excitement. After things settled down, they offered my son money, but Michael refused to take it. At first I even thought he was crazy. He could have paid off his student loan for culinary school. Why should this have surprised me though. This was consistent with the character of the young man I had raised. A distinctive quality which truly made me proud.

His good friend Jill told me that "Michael always said there was not enough time to do all that he wanted to do". One evening while Mike and Jill were hanging out together they decided to start asking each other about all their likes and dislikes and proceeded to write them down. Michael do you believe in reincarnation? Yes, I believe I've been here many times. This is my final great time. I'm here either to have a child and that child will be something great or I will be something great and do something that will make me famous.

Michael, what is your favorite color? My favorite color is blue.

And what about your favorite food? I like fusion, Japanese and French.

Favorite cooking show? East Meets West.

Favorite television personality? Oprah

Favorite author? Gary Zukav

Favorite color for a car? Black

Favorite opera singer? Andrea Bocelli

Favorite fast food? McDonald's and Taco Bell

Favorite Sandwich? Boneless rib from the corner deli

Favorite snack? Pretzels

Favorite drink? 7 & 7 for awhile

Favorite poem? The Road Not Taken

Favorite baseball team? The New York Mets

Michael, how do you want your body laid to rest? I don't know. I guess if I went before my parents they would lay me out and bury me. I don't need any of that . This body, it's just a body - it's a vessel. Our souls are what is really important. Once we die our soul is already gone. We're attached to our bodies now. I would want to be cremated. There is no use for my remains.

Jill was our next door neighbor, but before she moved in Vinny lived next door and on September 11, 2002 he wrote a letter to me which I must say was the first time in a year that I laughed. This is some of what Vinny had to say. "Michael was one of my first idols. Although we were different ages and did not hang out often, I still have many memories of him that pass through my mind every time I look at his picture. I remember one evening across the street at P.S.32 night center, Mike took Eric, Darren and myself to the little strip of grass on the outside of where the gym is. It was winter, so snow was on the ground. He told us if we could get him down, he would give us each ten dollars. After ten minutes of trying, he had a bloody nose and the three of us, besides being exhausted, were bruised and banged up and walking away. But with your son as my role model, I sure as hell wasn't about to quit. Picture this: it's night time, the ground is covered with snow, Mike is standing victorious - three kids who just had the s--t knocked out of them are limping away in defeat - the champion of the royal rumble is standing on the far side of the grassy strip wiping his nose with a handful of snow and I stop, turn around, face him and say you haven't won yet, I want that ten bucks (I must have been 13 or 14 years old and in case you don't recall, I was a short and fat pudgeball). So here comes a human butterball turkey charging full speed at a whole 3 wobbly mph towards your giant bull bastard of a son who had muscles in places nobody knew the human anatomy could have muscles. Mike sees me coming and instead of bracing for the tackle, bends down, puts his head between my stubby legs for leverage and flips me. When I tell you I must have gone 8-10 ft. in the air, I am not exaggerating. So the first words from Eric and Darren's mouth to each other are "HOLY S---T, DID YOU JUST SEE HIM FLIP VINNY?" I must have layed on the ground for ten minutes staring wide eyed at the snowy night sky in disbelief. In disbelief because I brought Mike down!!! Mike said it didn't count because he fell down laughing. Nancy I loved Michael and I hope I can grow up not just physically, but totally, to be a fraction of as great a man as Michael."

CHAPTER 7

After September 11, 2001 the thought of never seeing my son again was extremely heartbreaking. It didn't seem possible. And what I needed to do was to drown myself in everything "Michael". For a while I felt almost guilty as if maybe he may come home one day and think that I was snooping. But every day, there was something I explored of his while sitting on the floor in his room. Somehow it just brought me close to Michael. It prevented me from letting go. Something I certainly did not want to do.

One of the things I found was a letter which Michael wrote at the age of 12 to Mets catcher Gary Carter. I had no idea he had ever written it.

> Dear Gary,
>
> Hi, what's up? My name is Mike D'Auria. I live in Staten Island. I'm 12 and play for Great Kills Little League. I've been catching for 3 years. My coaches have great potential. I know it's only Little League but we still go through a lot. People don't know how hard it is, but I do.
>
> I love the Mets. My favorites are Keith Hernandez, Darryl Strawberry and especially you. You're my idol and your the best no matter what anyone says.
>
> When I grow up I want to be just like you. I was wondering if you could give me some advice, and I want yours, not the people that read these letters.
>
> Your the best.
>
> > `Your best fan,
> >
> > Michael D'Auria
>
> let's go Mets

During that period of time that found me sitting and reading through Michael's things I came across two letters written to a friend who my son believed he had so much in common with. Copies of the letters were returned to Michael because he had hoped one day to make a library of what he wrote and what he read.

> Due to "unworthy" misinterpretations unconsciously imbedded within the psyche, we, without awareness, allow rain to fall ever so slightly upon our parade - just enough to point out the negative disturbances. This we feel is self inherited through our own growth process. "Why me dejavu". The only difference in your case is that somewhere around 75% of this, rain hasn't even happened yet – in fact it's only partly cloudy. With you it's mere projection based upon youthful disappointments. Almost certain that something has to go wrong, this has taught you to conjure up the worst possible situation and place it on a shelf in the back of your head. There's no fault involved, only conditioning. The only unconditioning is to unconditionally love the beautiful positive parade. Don't pay attention to the clouds, just keep marching.
>
> > Love, Me

The beauty that God unfolds in our lives, is so beyond our full understanding, intwined within an intricately perfect plan, with just the right ingredients. As children with our physical temptations, unconscious capacity and curious wonder we lie in the midst. With any and all places to go. One sign of a soul on the path to spiritual enlightenment is to see the whole from a higher perspective and not allow ourselves to fall victim to false interpretations given by the mental. To rise to a higher call and heed what is needed to take the most out of the situation. As children it is so easy to selfishly allow a great thing to happen without regard for the greatness hidden. I've been good at a lot of things. I feel it's time to be great in this world.

I invite you to a place where greatness fits all facets, and questions can be answered. Where and when that place is will be determined as we go - so steady ahead in the timeless moment and allow yourself to be brilliant, gorgeous, talented and fabulous. Actually who are you not to be? You are a child of God.

Love, Me

It's amazing how you think you know your children and you really don't. I knew about the caring and courageous young man but I did not realize the depth of his intelligence and the impact he had on his friends' lives. How blessed am I to have brought this being into the world and be able to say he was MY son. But the loss of a child can put you in a place where you may never come back from.

So I needed to figure out how to move on after the death of Michael, my baby boy. Many people actually approached me after September 11 and made the statement "I don't know how you are handling it, I know I couldn't". Well guess what? I didn't think I could survive it either, but you do. You see, what's the alternative? I can move forward and make my son proud of me and be there for my daughter and family (who are also hurting) or I can't.

Michael was so full of life. He travelled, spent time in the city at the best restaurants, partied at the clubs and never let anything stop him from enjoying life. Why would I do anything different. And how could I withdraw when I still had another child. Christina was only 29 years old, married only a couple of years and just found out she was pregnant. She deserved me in her life as did her family. I also had my niece and five nephews ranging in age from six to seventeen years old. They were struggling on how to deal with the death of their cousin. I love them all too much to give them more heartache.

There were letters written by Michael to his cousin Robert letting him know the various steps he would go through in life as a young man. Another reason for us to believe he had some idea he would not be around to tell Robert himself. After September 11, Robert gave me a copy of three of those letters and I thought by reading a couple of them it would help you to get to know who my son was. I have to believe that since Robert only gave me these three letters that the rest he felt the need to keep private.

Robert,

Hey Cuz! Congratulations! I want you to know I'm honored to be your sponsor for confirmation. I'm writing this letter for a couple of reasons:

1)It's easier to understand than if I sat down and talked to you because you can go back and reread it whenever you want, until you understand my advice.

2) When I was younger I had a hard time being myself around my older cousins. I want you to be by yourself, in your own frame of mind when you read my letters.

There will be at least seven other letters during the next two years. Each one will be about different topics I feel a guy must know and understand to grow up. Growing up I never had anyone around to give me solid advice. My father left when I was 14 and I couldn't communicate with my older cousins. I had to figure things out on my own. That's something you don't want to have to do.

I'm sure no matter what anyone tells you (especially your parents) you're going to do what you feel you have to do, even though you may be wrong. I want to help you along. Simply to give you true advice and information about life. What you want to do with that advice is solely up to you. But if you want me to help you, you have to promise me you will be 100% honest with me. Because, we can talk about things all day, but if you're not honest, that talk won't mean a thing. We have to keep a level of respect and honesty. Even though you might think I'll get mad. Believe me there is nothing you can tell me that will get me mad at you.

The next eight years of your life are the most fun. They are also the hardest in a sense. There are seven key subjects you have to understand as best as you can to make it to my level.

1) self
2) friends
3) sex
4) money
5) drugs/temptation
6) goals
7) family

All of these things are connected to each other in one way or another. They all fit together like a puzzle. Your job is to collect as many pieces as you can and hopefully with my help put them in the right place. The closer you get to understanding where all the pieces go the stronger your upperhand will be over anyone else your age.

If you didn't understand that or anything else in this letter don't be afraid to ask me to explain.

LOVE YA CUZ

Michael

Robert,

FAMILY

The first thing I could tell you about family is that they are the most complex people to figure out.

Your mom and dad may seem like they are in control of life but they are just two kids that became older. They have a great deal of experiences with certain things but for the most part they are still trying to figure themselves out. Your parents are naturally the closest link you have to being on this earth. Therefore, they are the most important people. They are people that through the years have been through a lot of changes. You must remember that your mom and dad weren't always the same people you know now. They had a childhood and went through the same kinds of things you go through. But somehow time changes people's personalities. Time also makes you forget how it was to be young.

There may be a time in your life that you will discover "secrets" about their life. You may not like those things but you must remember that they didn't always know right from wrong. You can not blame them or bottle up mixed emotions about them; because like I've told you before, people are on their own when it comes down to it.

Dealing with who your parents are as people and who you came from is a very crucial situation in life. As long as your parents give you love and try to do the correct thing for you, you must respect them and give them the fulfillment in knowing they raised you right.

The advice on this whole page goes for aunts, uncles and other adults in your life. Your brothers, unfortunately, I can't give you an opinion on. I never had that bond of brotherhood in my life. That is something which I understand is priceless. From what I've seen, brothers are supposed to have a bond that no one can come between. They might do you wrong but don't you ever take someone else's side over your brothers'. Don't you ever let anyone abuse or take advantage of either of them. Cuz - this is the only thing that you can do to make me mad at you.

As far as your intermediate family - use your judgment. I'm sure they will always try to do the best for you. You should always give them their respect no matter what. You will know who you can trust more from your intuition. Cuz, I have to ask you a favor, you have to let cousin Stefanie know that she can come to you with a problem and you will be there to protect her.

As far as everyone else in your long extensive family you will truly take a liking to only 2 or 3 people. You must always be courteous and respectful to everyone else. Don't ever put anyone down, especially in front of another family member.

Your family can be the worst group of people you meet in your life, but this one is not like that. I have been given love and knowledge from each and every person in this family in one way or another.

A family with love is what keeps people together. They are the most important people you know. You must not ever disrespect any member whether you love them or hate them. This family will always be there if you need them - remember that.

Cuz, I'll make a pact with you. Since I never had a brother and always wanted one, would you fill that blank space for me? In return I will vow on everything holy that I will be there for you for any reason at any time, wherever we are. Write me a letter and tell me what you think.

I love you Cuz,
Michael

Robert,

SELF-YOURSELF

Throughout life there will be over 10,000 things that will throw you off track (make you lose sight of reality). One of the strongest things to prevent a lot of these bad experiences is a firm understanding of who Robert Perretta is.

From time to time throughout different stages, your opinion of who you are will change. That is normal. In fact believe it or not, you will never fully understand who you really are. Finding new things out about yourself and surprising yourself is what ultimately makes you become yourself. {This might not make a lot of sense but the more you read it the more you will understand it.}

Whether you realize it or not the people around you everyday affect you. Negatively or positively. Example: How many times have you made up a bullshit story just so your friends would think you were a little bit cooler. Everybody does that - that's a negative effect, when you try to be more than you are. After a while you start believing it.

A positive effect would be when you let someone else think they're a little bit better than you - when inside you know they're bullshitting. Don't make it obvious. For you to stay one step ahead of the next guy, you must let them think they are the shit. This gives you a huge advantage. {I'm getting a little ahead of myself - let me back track}. If you want to be strong you have to question yourself. Meaning: take time out at night , alone and think about your life right now. Ask yourself how you feel about certain things that are going on. Be honest when you answer your questions. If you can't truly be honest to yourself how can you ever trust any one else? This exercise will enable you to understand certain things about yourself. *Don't go crazy analyzing it though. Be brief and honest.

Somewhere along the way you will develop a respect for yourself that is so strong no one can break it. This respect must not only be mental. You have to develop a respect for your body as well. When you respect yourself like that people see it. And you will gain their respect as well - the right way, without having to play yourself. Once you have a good understanding of yourself you're half way there.

Limits - You have to know your limits. What kinds of things will I be faced with; will I be able to be in control of the situation. {think ahead, it keeps you sharp}. You must set these limits at where you're comfortable with them; and you must not be pressured by anyone (even yourself) to cross them. Very important - *Don't overstep your boundaries.

You have a loving family and live in a healthy environment. There are a lot of people who will do anything for you. ESPECIALLY ME. Keep that in mind - but at the same time please listen to my words. *You came into this world by yourself and you will leave by yourself. You are the only person you will ever totally have to yourself, everyone else is on their own.

You may be in love, you may have and trust a best friend, you may have Tommy and John, but each one is their own person and you must believe me, you can never change them! Only yourself, because you have control of it. Remember and please believe that cuz.

The final thing is just as important. Love, respect and trust in yourself without being self centered. Do not just put yourself before anyone else. You must learn to combine all of these things and still treat other people as you want to be treated. Those are not my words, they're God's words, and they make you gain so much out of life.

If you can control all of these things about your life, you have taken the first and biggest step into a beautiful happy life>that sounds gay but one day you will appreciate those words.

Cuz, I know I have jumped around a lot in this letter. I'm sorry, that's just how the thoughts flowed out of my mind. But, the more you read certain sections the more you will understand it. Take your time if you don't totally understand all that I've written, it will eventually come to you and you can <u>always</u> ask me. Don't be embarrassed. *Believe me there isn't anything that you can tell me that will make me angry because I have probably done the same things at least once before > that is the truth.

Good luck in whatever you may do.

I love you,

Michael
I'm here any time for you Robert.

This is a picture of the tattoo of Michael , that Robert had done, after Michael's death.

CHAPTER 8

Michael, My Brother

My first memory I have with Michael was the first time I held him in my arms. We were in the lobby of the hospital of which this great man was born. The journey of my childhood with Michael was fun and playful. He was my best friend growing up. We did have a good childhood and when a little older in our youth we began to grow a little apart since I was a girl and he a boy. But always through our childhood on into our teenage life Michael always stood by my side and defended me as though he were my older brother. In fact there were many people who thought he was. I must say that that was the very special way our relationship was. I always felt maternal and he felt like he had to be by my side like an honorable young man. To give you an example of a young man so brave and heart driven, I recall a day at my girlfriend's home when some 17 and 18 year old guys came ringing the doorbell threatening us. I called Michael and he came running barefoot to my girlfriend's to protect us from those guys. They were gone when he arrived. I don't know how many thirteen year olds would do such an act for their older sister.

There is much that is so personal but as a young man, especially during the time of our parents divorce, Michael did have some emotional turmoil going on but always managed to be spiritual and prosper on. Tattooing became a part of who he was. I believe it kept him in perspective. I always felt like Michael and I were twins and as an adult he had the same feeling as I did which he told me once in a heart to heart I hold so dear to me. My story with him is so dramatic. We did live apart for so many years of our lives. I was eighteen years old and he was fourteen when I graduated from high school and moved out to go to school in Manhattan. One year later I moved back home and that was when Michael moved to Florida to be with our dad. Although we did not see each other all the time I was still so emotionally drawn to his emotional world. Without a word I felt his happiness, grief, confusion, or anger. We then grew accustomed to appreciating the moments we spent together on holidays and getting together at the dining room table at mom's house. I danced with Michael to the song "Through the Years" at my wedding. He told me he was truly proud to have this dance with me on such a wonderful occasion. I wouldn't have it any other way. My agony measures my love and pride for Michael.

Michael's best, what he could have done, we'll never know. But what he did accomplish, many will never. I was so proud of my brother. When it came to his fire department tests and becoming a chef I realized how ambitious he really was. It was very hard to be focused at times but he was determined more than anyone I know.

One night, while watching a commercial on television, it reminded me to call my brother. It was 11 pm. I phoned him and thinking I might get his answering machine I was pleasantly surprised to hear his voice. We were having a wonderful conversation on the phone, when Mike said, "This is ridiculous. We live five minutes away from one another, I'll pick up a six pack and be right over." I was so happy and anxious, I eagerly awaited. My husband Christopher had fallen asleep, and the rest of the night Mike and I sat on the floor across from one another. We were really having fun. We had some of the most fabulous conversations. Till this day certain words are so vividly captured by my memory. Michael asked me, "What do you think the meaning of your life is here?" I said to him it's not who I will be but who my children will be. Michael replied, "When I die it's going to be in a big way and it will change the world". How ironic.

The end of June, 2001, Michael completed his fire department training on Randall's Island. Family day on Randall's Island was to show the families their training skills. It was such a proud day. We were in the auditorium with the rest of the families to watch a film on what it meant to be a firefighter. My mom asked Michael two times when graduation day was. He said to us "Today is my graduation day, my family is here". And for him it was because physically he did not graduate. Somehow I am so happy it felt to him to be his graduation day. It meant so much to him to have us by his side on such an important occasion in his life. After Family Day we did not see much of each other. My husband and I bought our first home in June of 2001 and Michael came over to see it and promised Christopher he would do all he could to help him work on it.

The last memory I have of Michael physically in my presence was when we had family over for a labor day barbecue. Michael showed up a little later on because he was working. He was wearing his black and white FDNY teeshirt from my uncle's firehouse. We were having such a good time. I was sitting a seat away from Michael with my cousin Stefanie in between us. I asked Stef to switch seats with me and automatically Michael said with amusement "Oh, my sister misses me. She wants to sit next to me." He was so right. At that point our picture was taken with Robert and Stefanie standing behind us. It was our last picture together. I was so happy that day, but the picture told a different story. I looked sad. Not long after the picture Michael said he needed to go home and get some sleep since he was working the next morning. The last hug I had with my brother was in my kitchen. I remember so clearly, besides saying goodbye, I told him "I love you, I miss you, I'm proud of you".

The morning of September 11, 2001, I awoke crying from a dream I had. I got ready for work and when I arrived at work I read my horoscope. It read "Today's the day that will change your life forever". Watching TV in the corner of the restaurant where I worked I saw the first plane hit the North Tower. Then the second plane hit. I went into the restroom and started to pray. All I kept thinking about is Michael at the World Trade Center. He had to be there because he was a Manhattan Firefighter. I felt like he was in danger. I called my mom to see if he was working and she confirmed my worst fears. Michael was working. After I got off the phone I was freaking out saying my brother's in trouble. Then the South Tower collapsed. I fell to the floor crying and screaming. I got up and ran outside the back door of the restaurant and screamed Michael's name at the top of my lungs. I knew it. I felt it.

My husband picked me up from the restaurant and we went directly to the local hospital to donate blood, then went to my mom's home. Needless to say it was agony not hearing from Michael. He did not own a cell phone. We kept trying to think positively. We called the Manhattan area hospitals to see if he was there but his name was not on any list. They kept telling us "unaccounted for".

It was three and a half long months but my family was fortunate to have Michael's remains identified. January 1, 2002 at 12 midnight Michael's alarm clock went off. At 1:30 am, just one and a half hours later my brother was found.

My first child, Vanessa Michael, was born in August, 2002 at 3:43 am. So we know Michael was with us. You see, there were 343 firefighters who died on 9/11. That was the sign I needed to know that my brother was with me. My second child, Adrianna Rose, was born February, 2006. Both my girls know who Uncle Mike is. Not only by my doing or my mom's. Vanessa has played hide and seek with Uncle at the age of two.

Adrianna, barely one, would go over to a table of pictures and kiss Michael's picture, while other pictures of family members sat there, no one saying a word to her. She recently pointed to a picture of the World Trade Center and said "fell down".

My children will always know the hero that died before they were born. And how lucky are they? He is their uncle. Always watching over them. As for me, well, I am the luckiest sister. I had an extraordinary brother. He had a deep sense of spirituality and kindness, not to mention a brave person who I know was a true warrior. I told Michael the week before I got married as I held his face "I love you so much I would die for you". I truly meant it. I miss the belly laughs. My brother, the comedian. Always turned a conversation into a joke. Michael had the best hug ever. His embrace always made me feel safe. He had the best shoulder to cry on. A true listener. A true inspiration. He died. He died for me and my family. He died for all that is good. He died for peace. This is the man that I was so blessed to have had in my life. My brother, my only sibling.

CHAPTER 9

When Michael moved to Florida to live with his father for that one year, my mom and dad, Michael's maternal grandparents had had a condominium just one mile away. That comforted me knowing that they were there for him at that time.

When my son was younger though, Grandma remembers teaching him how to play the card game "Uno" and how bad he felt if he would win and she would lose. But even earlier than that, she recalls one Thanksgiving day, just as we were about ready to sit and eat dinner, Michael was found under the table untying his great uncle's shoe laces and then retying them. Only this time he tied the left shoe to the right shoe. Of course Uncle John knew what was going on but did not want to spoil his fun.

On one of his many vacations to Florida, Michael went to visit his grandparents who just happened to be there at the same time. My mom talked Michael and his friend into leaving their laundry and she would do it for them. Five wash to be exact. She did not know that they needed the clothes the same evening and when they came back to pick them up my parents weren't home, since they went to a dinner/dance. First he tried to climb in the kitchen window. By the way they were on the second floor. Then he found their friend who worked on the Board of Directors and had the key. She let them in the apartment, she thought just to get their clothes. But instead, my son sat her down on the recliner and put the television on for her while he and his friend took showers, gathered their clean clothes and then left with her. My mom laughs and calls it an unforgettable fiasco.

On Sunday, September 9, 2001, back in Staten Island, New York, mom came upstairs to use our scale to weigh herself. Michael was home and since she had forgotten her eyeglasses, she called him to have him read the scale for her. "Little did I know that would be our last moment together."

Michael was the second grandchild in our family, Christina being the first. But she was so sweet just as a little girl would be. Michael on the other hand, well that was another story. When he was very young my dad remembers watching a football game on television, lying on the living room floor with Michael stepping over him. When grandpa asked Michael to stop he asked if he could just do it one more time. Since he remembered how his grandfather would tease him endlessly, it was time for payback. So he pounced on grandpa's stomach and shut the television set off at a very crucial time in the game. They both started to laugh and then proceeded to wrestle. With the blonde hair Michael had as a little boy, he reminded my dad of the cartoon character Joe Palooka so dad would refer to Mike as Joe Palooka, Jr.

When my son was around twelve years old dad would take him on occasion to football practice and games. On every play Michael would fight like heck to get to the quarterback and many times did so. Since he enjoyed football dad later took him to see the New York Giants.

At the age of fourteen dad and mom remember taking Mike out to dinner. Knowing how Michael loved shrimp they waited to hear what he wanted to order. When Michael saw the price he chose something else. My parents ordered the shrimp for him anyway. That same year, while mom and dad were back in Florida, and Michael was living with his dad, my parents would go to all of Michael's baseball games at Boyd Anderson High where he had been the catcher. The team did not fair too well that year, but Michael was always hustling and yelling at the pitchers and infielders to "talk it up". My parents recall hearing a dad in the stands remark "if everybody hustled like the catcher we would win more games".

Several years later when Michael first became a firefighter he bought a Jeep. This Jeep had a hard top that could be removed. Dad spent many hours with Michael struggling to remove the top and had a few good laughs over it. "That time we spent alone will always remain with me."

"Since Michael is gone there is such a void in our lives. We will never be the same - yet we are so much better off for having had him in our lives." These are my sister Angela's words. She goes on to say how Michael was more than a nephew. She would jokingly call Michael and Christina her "practice children". Angela remembers going with my son on a boy scout trip to a pumpkin patch. She took him to work on occasion and even to the movies and to get chinese food. Coloring Easter eggs was another fun memory for her.

As she had her own children, she would watch Michael become a big brother to them, sleeping over and playing with them. Putting together toys for them on Christmas day and ultimately becoming a role model. As he got older and his life busier how thrilled she was when ever she got the chance to see him always hoping he would be there when visiting my home. If he was not she would leave him a note to say "hi". "To this day when I see a can of Redi-Whip I think of Michael with a mouthful."

Michael was always up to something, says Aunt Lucille. When he was young he would busy himself either under the table, juggling fruit, or doing magic tricks. As an adult he was still a big kid, always looking to make you laugh. "We had to hide desserts from him, especially Aunt Angela's seven layer cookies or there would be none left for dessert."

One of my brother Robert's special memories was when he transferred to his new firehouse, Engine 234, and Michael, at six and a half years old came to help him carry his gear upstairs to his new locker. At thirteen years old he spent a 15 hour tour and rode the Engine on all the calls. Robert recalls how Michael loved the "great food" and the chance to eat any time he wanted.

After September 11, Robert along with our brother-in-law Bobby, a fire lieutenant, had the excruciating task of having to empty my son's locker at his firehouse. Bobby was also my family member called on January 1, 2002 and told Michael was found. He, in turn, called my brother who was retired at that point. After Michael was officially identified by his dental records that day, it was my family again who came to my home to hold my hand and cry with me.

When he was around six or seven years old I remember hugging Michael this one particular day. You know how soft and cuddly small children can be. For some reason that moment was more special than others and I remember saying to myself "never forget what this feels like". I never did. And every so often throughout Michael's life and even now I remember that moment and how special it was.

On my birthday only a couple of years before our great loss I received a phone call from my son to wish me a Happy Birthday. I knew he was working that day and was unable to get off. But to my surprise as we talked he was heading up my stairs, a large hazelnut birthday cake, which he had made for me, in his hands. He took the night off from work to be with me. After putting down the cake, he went over to our stereo and put a tape in of a song called "Mama" by Boyz to Men and danced with me in my living room.

This is the young man I bore, raised and loved for almost twenty six years. You wonder why some days you get by being able to smile, laugh or just talk about the child you lost and why other days are so gut wrenchingly unbearable. Then there are the times I can easily talk about my Michael with a smile on my face and then feel guilty later for not crying.

Michael used to say to me "Mom, you worry too much". Now I hear him say "Mom, be happy". So I remember my son's big bright smile and all the times he made me crazy as a teen and I must look back and smile. I've been told so many heartwarming stories about the young man I thought I knew so well but got to know even better after he was gone. I often told Michael how proud I was of him and how much I loved him. Today that gives me peace.

Printed in the United States
by Baker & Taylor Publisher Services